GW00457929

TESTIMONIES

(SCOTLAND 1623–1965)

BY THE SAME AUTHOR

Morgan & Me, A Memoir, Happen*Stance*, 2020
Paper Cut, Shoestring Press, 2020
Things We Never Knew, Shoestring Press, 2016
Now the Robin, Happen*Stance*, 2018
Hannah, Are You Listening? Happen*Stance*, 2013
The Unswung Axe, Shoestring Press, 2012
A Bird in the Hand, Shoestring Press, 2008
Window on the Garden, Essence Press/Botanic Press, 2006
Siva in Lamlash, minimal missive, 1991
Rooms, Aquila Press, 1986
apple on an orange day, Autolycus Press, 1973

As editor:
Edwin Morgan, Centenary Selected Poems, Carcanet 2020

ACKNOWLEDGEMENTS

I should like to thank poets Stewart Conn, Liz Lochhead
and Jane McKie for their encouragement of this project.

First published in 2022 by Happen*Stance* Press
21 Hatton Green, Glenrothes KY7 4SD
https://happenstancepress.com

ISBN: 978-1-910131-71-8

Printed & bound by Imprint Digital, Exeter
https://digital.imprint.co.uk

TESTIMONIES

(SCOTLAND 1623–1965)

Poems

Hamish Whyte

HAPPENSTANCE PRESS

CONTENTS

[*cont.*]

I have long been an admirer of the American poet
Charles Reznikoff (1894-1976) and particularly his great
work, *Testimony: the United States (1885-1915)*, which
was based on his reading of court records from several
USA states. It inspired me to do something similar for
Scotland.

Case by case, in Reznikoff's 'transcriptions', he never
gives the reader the outcome of the trials—there's no
verdict or sentence—it's the people, the voices, the
stories that are important. Here I have deviated from
this, sometimes including both verdict and sentence
and keeping to the original language of the trial reports
as much as possible—basically making 'found' poems.
Reznikoff also changed names and places. I have kept
the original names and places.

The pieces in the sequence are arranged chronologically
and are taken from reports of trials in Scotland from
the seventeenth to the twentieth century. These are lost
stories and voices found again and speaking to us down
the ages. They show us what we've always suspected—
that some things don't change.

H.W.

Thomas Gowdie, merchant in Dumfries,
was accused of killing Herbert McKie
on the last day of December at the brig-end
by giving him a great and deadly strike
with his foot in his secret parts, upon
his breast and on his left shoulder
whereby his shoulder bone was broken
out of joint. Of these strikes he never
convalesced but lay in his bed in great dolour
and pain and after twenty days he died
of the said hurts and wounds. Gowdie said
there was never quarrel or discord between him
and McKie for whose slaughter he is wrongly
and unjustly pursued.

'Within a few days the Devil came
to me in the New Wards of Inshoch
and there had carnal copulation
with me. He was a very large black
rough man. His member is exceeding great
and long; no man's member is so long
and big as his. He would be among us
like a loose horse among mares.
He would lie with us in preference
of all the multitude, neither had we or he
any kind of shame. He would lie
and have carnal copulation with all,
at every time, as he pleased. He would have
carnal dealing with us in the shape of a deer
or any other shape that he would be in.
We would never refuse him. He would come
to my house-top in the shape of a crow,
or like a deer, or in any other shape, now and then.
I would ken his voice at the first hearing of it,
and would go forth to him and have
carnal copulation with him. The youngest
and lustiest women have very great pleasure
in their carnal copulation with him, yes,
much more than with their ain husbands,
and they have an exceeding great desire
of it with him, as much as he can with them,
and more, and never think shame of it.
He is abler for us than any man can be,
only he was very heavy like a malt sack,
a huge nature, very cold, as ice.'

Margaret Whythill, spouse to James Love,
said she saw James Algie, a merchant, bring his wife
to the close mouth and throw her down
in the strand and saw her rise again
and follow him up the close and say,
'I'll never live with you, do to me what you please.'
She saw this happen three times.

Euphemia Perrie, aged forty-six years,
said she saw Algie struggling with his wife
on the stair head, and she, desiring to be in,
he would not suffer her, and desired her
to let him see what she had; and she
held out both her hands and said, 'I hae naethin.'
He would not let her go in and threw her
over the stair and she cried out,
'Will none help me, but suffer me to be murdered?'

The magistrates complained the Tolbooth
was pestered with many silly old women
who were a great charge to the town.
The Council ordered those
who were guilty of 'reset and converse'
to be whipped and burned on the cheek
and those who were guilty of 'bad principles'
to be whipped only.

John Thomson and Agnes Walkinshaw,
tenants in the farm of Pathhead, without any cause
or provocation, but probably from previous ill-will
towards one of their neighbours, Mrs Margaret Purdon,
entered her house and shaken of all fear of God,
fell upon the body and person of Margaret Purdon,
she being civilly sitting and spinning at the wheel
and gave her many sharp and bloody strokes on several
parts of her body, dang her to the ground, punching her
with feet and hands and other offensive weapons, so that
if it had not been the providence of God and help
of good neighbours, they had without doubt bereaved her
of her good life.

Alexander Stuart escaped hanging
by accepting perpetual servitude
in the silver mines of Glen Ochil.
Round his neck he wore an iron collar
inscribed *Alexander Stuart found guilty*
of theft at Perth and gifted by the justiciars
as perpetual servant to Sir J. Erskine of Alloa.
This collar was later found in the River Forth
where he had probably drowned himself.

There were two rival shoemakers
in the same village, William Hamilton and John Blair,
who had no kindly feelings between them
and vented their hostility in outrageous conduct
and in abuse of each other.

On the sixteenth of June, under cloud of night,
Blair and his spouse came to the Hamiltons' house
and threw several stones at the windows
breaking many of them, and threatened
Hamilton and his family to come out
for their lives if they dared, that they would
rive their souls and burn them and burn
their house above their heads and make
the highest stone the lowest and called
his wife and family whores and thieves.

John Neilson owned a game cock
of an extraordinary brood, which was coveted
by his neighbour James Brown, a cooper,
who had a taste for cock-fighting.
The cock, having strayed, was picked up
by Brown; to enable him to keep possession
he attempted to prevent it being identified
by pulling and clipping its feathers and cutting
its comb, changing its appearance.
The following year this wonderful bird
somehow got out of Brown's hands
and returned to its owner's premises,
but Brown came and took it away and again
kept and detained it, although he had no title to.

William Wilson of Mains, in Eastwood Parish,
courted a Miss Ferguson but failed to win the consent
of her friends to their marriage, so he took her off to Edinburgh,
where, in the Canongate, in a clandestine and irregular way,
he was married to his lady-love by a person not authorised
by the Kirk, and cohabited with her and owned her for his wife.

For this he was fined one hundred merks
and jailed for three months. The fine was put
to the repair of Rouken Bridge (which happened
to be near Wilson's residence) and anything left over
was given to the poor.

James Moody, innkeeper,
was summoned before the sheriff
by Robert Ewing for payment
of a debt of £8 due by bill.
Moody denied he owed more than £4
and alleged the bill had been fraudulently
obtained from him when the worse of drink.
Moody gave one juror ten shillings,
promising more if he got off, and to another
he offered the occasional use, free of hire,
of a horse.

To the tuck of a drum
Jean Montgomery, convicted of stealing linen
from a bleaching field, was led, stripped to the waist,
through the streets by the public executioner
who flogged her at intervals
before taking her to jail.

On the 11th of August the ship Blackgrove
laden with cargo came in to the Clyde
and when near Greenock a boat was put out

from the shore and into it some goods were removed
from the ship, for the purpose of being smuggled and
the duties evaded. This being observed by Hugh McLachlan,

a boatman belonging to a wherry at Inverkip
in the revenue service, he, along with Archibald Stewart,
John McIntyre, Hector McPhail and Archibald Bell,

four other revenue boatmen, went out in the wherry
in order to make a seizure of the smuggled goods;
and having gone alongside the vessel

they were assailed with great violence and with sticks
and stones, struck, wounded and bruised
by John Lade, elder, of Quarter, his son John,

James Morris of Quarter, his son Hugh,
and James Glen of Bankhead: whereby
Hugh McLachlan was killed, John McIntyre's arm

was broken and McPhail, Stewart and Bell
were cut, wounded and bruised. The assailants
were forced to fly and abscond.

On the 19th of March, a Sabbath, between
eleven and twelve o'clock, William Oak, weaver
in Johnstone, Thomas Potts, weaver in Williamsburgh,
Paisley, William Pullans and George Aitcheson,
weavers in Irvine, all Irishmen, broke into
the house of John Barr, farmer, of Gryffe Castle
in the parish of Houston, armed with bludgeons,
large knives, cutlasses or swords. The female servant
was the first to get up, and she acted the part
of heroine on the occasion. The ruffians
brandished their weapons over the heads of the inmates,
threatening to take the life of Barr, and, with horrid
oaths and imprecations, demanded money
and the keys of the repositories. They robbed
the house of £11 in notes, £1 in silver,
and some silver spoons. The spoil was carried
to Oak's house and divided among the robbers.
Potts had been previously charged with other crimes
and the large knife with which he was armed at the robbery
was discovered concealed in a barrel about his premises.

While the ballot for a jury was taking place
George Jamieson, baker, Pleasance, on his name being called
stated that on account of certain religious scruples
he could not take the necessary oath. He had been
of the Antiburgher persuasion but had left
because he disapproved of covenanting.
The Lord Justice-Clerk said he could not be exempted.
Jamieson was firmly resolved not to take the oath.
The Lord Justice-Clerk bade him go home and read his Bible,
in which he would find no warrant for such scruples.

Sentencing two youths, John McLeod, chair-maker,
and Alexander Shaw, cabinet-maker, for stealing
a silver hunting-watch, a gold chain and seals,
the judges stated that it was a melancholy case,
from the youth of the prisoners. In morality and expediency,
considering them incorrigible, they could propose
no punishment short of transportation for fourteen years.
Day after day they had the melancholy spectacle
of boys entering on life, placed at their bar.
It was a mournful proof of the immorality of the age;
and they sincerely wished that the large sums
expended on missionary and other foreign societies
were applied at home in procuring moral and religious
instruction for unfortunate children, neglected,
or altogether deserted, by their natural guardians.

On the 20th of June on the highway
from Edinburgh to Musselburgh
Robert Reid drove a coach and two horses
against and over Robert Stretton, a private
in the 1st Dragoon Guards, who there was reason
to believe was drunk, whereby the wheels
passed over his legs and body
and he was severely and mortally wounded
and languished until the 22nd of June
when he died.

William Campbell, nine years old,
was convicted of housebreaking
by means of false keys.
The witness against his masters
who had supplied the keys
failed to appear in court and they
were let off.
Campbell was sentenced to eighteen
months in prison and to be kept
at hard labour.

On the morning of 23rd July
William Buist and George Jervice
broke into the public house in South Leith
known as Jock's Lodge, owned by William Bowden,
by forcing open one of the windows,
and stole four pork hams weighing from ten
to fifteen pounds each, four plated candlesticks,
a double Gloucester cheese
and twelve pounds of tea.

John Thomson, a brushmaker from Portobello,
was waiting for a coach on North Bridge,
pacing up and down, holding in his hands
a pair of new shoes, neatly wrapped.
He told the police he was perfectly sober
and that a woman had come up to him
and taking hold of his coat front in a gentle manner
had said, 'My dear, what are you going to give me
tonight.' He sent her off but as she was leaving
he felt his watch being pulled from its pocket
so he grabbed her. She gave him a great deal
of abusive language; a crowd gathered;
she threw the watch down and Thomson let go
of her to pick it up; a young man stepped forward
and restrained the woman, an English pickpocket,
whose name was Hannah Barton.

EDINBURGH, 1828

A crazy chair stood by the fireplace
near two broken wooden stools;

old shoes and implements for shoemaking
lay scattered on the floor; a pot

full of boiled potatoes and broken glass
with old rags and straw were near a cupboard

on which were some plates and spoons;
the bed was a coarse wooden frame

without posts or curtains and was filled
with old straw and rags. Among them

a man's shirt, stained with blood in front,
and something like a child's shift,

also bloody, were plainly discernible.
At the foot of the bed, between it and the wall,

was a heap of straw under which
the woman's body had been concealed. The bed

stood so near the wall that the corpse
must have been doubled up.

GLASGOW, 1840

A climbing boy
scarcely eight years old
was compelled by threats
to go up or down
thirty-eight new chimneys
in succession
with no interval
for rest or food.
The labour and danger
were increased
by the amount of lime
and rubbish obstructing
the vents which
he had to clear
with a chisel.
Exhausted, cold,
wet and excoriated,
he died in the thirty-eighth
chimney. His master
was charged with
culpable homicide.
It was claimed he
had an affection
for the boy
and worked him
to death from no
anger or selfishness
but merely
from the general brutality
of his craft.

An otherwise respectable woman
accused of causing the death of her child
by neglect was so overcome by remorse
that she lost the use of her limbs
and had to wait three years to be tried,
by which time she had become very pious.
She was lifted like a big child into court
in the arms of a huge porter; after sentence
he put his left hand under her as a nurse
does to a child and (she steadying herself
by placing her right arm over his neck)
carried her away.

John Killocher, a young Irish labourer,
worked on the Scottish Central Railway,
lodging near Blackford with Jenny Anderson
who kept a refreshment shop and her son
who was the village blacksmith.
Four years later Killocher was back
in the neighbourhood and resolved
to pay a call. All were at church,
as it was a communion Sunday, except
the woman, who received him hospitably.
Thinking there was money in the house
he seized a hatchet and struck her several blows
then ransacked the house.

William Bennison married Mary Mullen
in the county of Armagh in Ireland,
but left her after a few months
and went to live in Paisley, Renfrewshire,
where he bigamously married Jane Hamilton,
but left her after a few weeks
and went back to his first wife in Ireland;
he then returned to Scotland
and lived with Jane Hamilton,
first in Paisley then in Edinburgh,
where, in a house in Leith Walk,
he gave her arsenic in her porridge
so that after two days of great suffering
she died.

Margaret McMillan and Elizabeth Layburn
shared a house with two other women.
There was a party one night with two bottles
of whisky. 'All were well enough,
but not drunk.' The next morning
a quarrel took place between McMillan
and Layburn, first in the kitchen,
then in the garden, where McMillan
lifted a stool or creepie and struck Layburn
on the head, who lifted up the stool
and said, 'She has done for me.'
She bled very much and was carried
into the house, but received no treatment.
She was seized six days after the blow
with lock-jaw and died the next day.
Medical men who examined her
said that if aid had been sought in time
the lock-jaw might not have followed,
though it might, even under
the most skilful treatment.

David Balfour, porter and pointsman
on the Edinburgh and Glasgow Railway,
whose duty it was to see and take care
that everything about the switches or points
under his charge at Garngaber,
where the Monklands Junction Railway joins
the Edinburgh and Glasgow Railway,
was right and in working order, and to keep
the same locked or shut, except when required
to be opened to admit of the passage of engines
or trains, appeared to have failed to shut or lock
a switch or point connected with a line of rails
leading into a siding, in consequence of which
a passenger train from Airdrie to Glasgow
was prevented from passing from the Monklands
Junction Railway on to the main line
of the Edinburgh and Glasgow Railway
and had its course diverted into the siding
and came violently in collision with a train
or number of trucks then standing in the siding,
whereby the passengers were violently thrown
against each other or against the carriages
and were cut, bruised and wounded
and put in danger of their lives, in particular:

Robert McLachlan, clerk to William Buist & Co.,
merchants in Airdrie, was cut and bruised on his face
and head; Ann McIlrevie or Boness, wife of Robert Boness,
contractor in Airdrie, was rendered insensible and had
one of her ribs fractured; Daniel McCormick,
collier's drawer from Rawyards in New Monkland,

had his right hand sprained and was otherwise bruised
and wounded; Barnard McIlhone, labourer, also
from Rawyards, had two of his teeth fractured and face
bruised; Barnard Kean, miner from Airdrie, was bruised
on his back; John Watt, shoemaker, also from Rawyards,
was rendered insensible; John Boyd, labourer, also
from Rawyards, was rendered insensible and had two
of his teeth fractured; Margaret Campbell or Connoway,
wife of John Connoway, miner from Aidrie, was rendered
insensible and severely cut above her right eye;
John Connoway also was severely cut across his brow;
John Allan, miner also from Rawyards, was cut on his leg;
Sarah McWilliam or Delargy, wife of James Delargy,
mason from Airdrie, was rendered insensible and was cut
and bruised on her face and head; David Mitchell,
clerk to James Thomson Rankine, writer in Airdrie,
was rendered insensible and cut and bruised on his face
and side; Ann McPherson or Sands, wife of James Sands,
wagon driver of Hall Craig, was cut and bruised on her head
and face; Robert Sands, collier's drawer, who lived
with his father and mother, was cut and bruised
on his face and other parts of his body.

Two brothers, Michael and Peter Scalan, from Mayo
were employed in the lime pits at Hilton of Forthar
and lodged next door to Margaret Maxwell
who kept a small shop. They owed her
some money and as they couldn't pay
she refused to give them further credit.
Out of revenge, one night they broke into her house
by the back window, dragged the woman
from her bed and smashed her skull to pieces.
They stole a silver watch, three pounds in cash
and a copy of the New Testament.

There was a fellow who hated his stepmother
so much that he said he would kill the child
she was expecting. He kept his word
by cutting off its head. His defence
was insanity and the judge said no doubt
he was as mad as gusts of passion
could make him, but not nearly mad enough
to cut off heads with impunity.

Alexander Cunninghame, about thirty-five,
a strong, resolute-looking scoundrel,
murdered his wife, a well-conditioned,
good woman who, with her four children,
had left him after numerous assaults.
He often said he would like to kill her
and would shoot her as easily as a seagull.
He found out where she was living
and borrowed a gun, powder and shot;
he went into the garden and saw her,
sitting, with a candle, at her loom;
he threw some gravel against the window
and when she looked up he fired.
At the trial he muttered to his counsel,
'If they hang me, whit'll they dae wi ma claes?'

The schooner *Nymph* left Montrose for London
carrying a cargo of flooring. The crew
were the captain, John Greig, and three seamen,
Pert, Rae and Andrew Brown.
Off the Forfar coast Brown attacked Greig
with an axe as he lay asleep in his bunk,
striking him two terrible blows to the head.
Pert rushed at Brown and prevented a third blow
by taking the axe and throwing it overboard.
When Pert asked Brown, 'What have you done?'
he said, 'Well, Jock, I am going stark mad,
out of my mind.' He said it was on account
of some former grudge. 'Will you come
and see me hanged? It is a good thing
you got the axe or you would have got the same.'
Brown took command of the ship and steered
it to Stonehaven, where his mother lived.
He said if anyone disobeyed his commands
he would be pitched overboard.
He was arrested at his mother's house.

'My name is Gavin Renwick. I live in Fairybank Cottage—
a room and kitchen. It stands by itself, about 90 yards
from my brother's house. I live alone generally.
On the evening of 12th October I went to bed as usual
in the kitchen about 9 o'clock. I secured the front door,
which I found broken the next morning. I was awakened
by a noise in the course of the night. I looked up, and rose,
and saw two men coming ben. One never came out of the dark.
One came forward to the fire and asked for spunks. I went
to the fire and took up the poker to stir it but he took the poker
before I could get my hand on it, except for a very little.
I knew the man and had done for years. After he took the poker
he knocked me down with a heavy iron instrument he had
in his hand and repeated the blows. There were 21 marks
of injuries upon me from what he did. I believe he meant
to kill me. I told him I knew him, whereupon he flew upon me
like a wild dog—I being an old man of 82. He seized me
by the throat and compressed it, trying to choke me,
leaving the black marks of his fingers on my throat.
I became insensible for nearly half an hour, so I did not see
the men taking the articles they took. I did not understand
anything for two days after this, I was so bad.'

The men took away from the house: a fowling piece,
a six chamber revolver, two metal powder flasks,
a leather shot bag, a shilling in bronze money, two
or thereby pairs of blankets, a linen sheet, a cotton sheet,
three cotton handkerchiefs, three or thereby pairs of trousers,
three or thereby vests, a silver watch with brass chain
and shell attached, and a pair of shoes.

One summer's day some boys were bathing
in a burn bounded on one side by the grounds
of Chapelhouse estate. A valuable collie dog
belonging to one of the boys followed him
into the burn and after some time
jumped out on the Chapelhouse bank
and ran about shaking and drying itself.
A rabbit started and the dog gave chase.
The rabbit got into a hole and the dog stood
and scraped at the mouth of the hole. The dog's master
repeatedly called it back, but it did not come.
In a short time Jack Campbell, coachman at Chapelhouse,
who also acted as a gamekeeper, came down the field
towards the dog with a gun and when about five yards
from the dog took aim and fired at it. The dog then went
to the burn and crossed it with evident pain.
It then lay down near the burn and the boys
took it home with difficulty and it tried to lie down
repeatedly on the way. The dog was still in great pain
for a considerable time after it was shot. The shot used
was ordinary No. 4 or 5 and at the place where the dog was shot
there were brambles and other cover for game.
Campbell said the dog was trespassing
and he wished to kill it outright
and with as little pain as possible.
His firing did not amount to cruelty.
The dog's owner said that firing was not necessary,
the dog could have been driven away with stones.
If the act was done with intention to injure
it amounted to wanton cruelty.

On Saturday the 14th of August the Irish Nationalist Association
held its annual gathering. Its members were marching
in procession through the city when they came into contact
with a crowd of Orangemen, among whom was a body of police,
numbering about sixty, several of whom were in plain clothes.
A fight ensued, with sticks, stones and other weapons
and the police used their batons.
Twenty persons of those in the Nationalist procession
were apprehended, including John O'Brien
who was accused of assaulting constable Henry Douglas
and constable Alexander McLeod. O'Brien claimed
he did not know they were constables
as they were in plain clothes.

Helen Thomson, aged twenty-four, drowned
her two-year-old illegitimate son Charles
by putting him head down in a butter-kit filled
with water in the washing house behind her house.
She had recently visited her mother who was
confined in the Fife and Kinross Lunatic Asylum.
Her mother had raged at her and said it was Helen
who had put her there. From that date
Helen became depressed, inattentive to her work,
and dirty and negligent in her dress and habits,
having previously been a clean and tidy woman.
The manager of the linen works where she was
employed said he had always looked upon her
as a woman of weak mind.

The publican Hugh Greenhill and his wife
left their hotel on Sunday afternoon,
leaving a girl Reid in charge. She seems to have acted
as a waitress; strict instructions were given to her
to admit and serve only bona fide travellers.
The only other person in the house was the cook.
And the publican before leaving gave some beer and whisky
to Reid in case any bona fide travellers should come.
None did come but two sweethearts of the girls,
said to be Sunday-school teachers, and well known
as not bona fide travellers, and to them
Reid supplied two glasses out of the bottle of whisky,
which was paid for by one of the men, and must have been
so paid in order to supply the plain deficit in the bottle;
for of course as the bottle was diminished by two glasses,
it had to be handed back to the publican as if the glasses
had been given to bona fide travellers; and it was so
handed back to him on his return home.

According to witnesses, William Henry Bury
rushed into the police station and shouted,
'I'm Jack the Ripper; if you go to my house
you will find the body of my wife, which I have cut up
and placed in a box.' The police went to the house
and found the body of Mrs Bury in a large packing case
in a horribly mutilated condition.
Bury had recently come to Dundee from the east end
of London where he was regarded as a bad character
and it was said that bloodstains had been found in his room.

John Carlin, a boatman from Govan, on the 7th of December
being on the Clyde on the outlook for an approaching vessel,
had occasion to obey a call of nature by passing urine
which he did standing up in his boat with his face
to the Partick side of the river, which was about 80 yards distant,
his back being to the Govan side, about 20 yards behind him.
He heard a voice shout to him from the Govan side
but on turning round saw no person near. Mary Smith
or O'Dwyer of Albert Street, Govan, laid a complaint
against him of wilfully, indecently and in a shameless manner
exposing his person to her.

Alexander Mackellar was accused
of sending to Daniel Goble, grocer,
the following threatening letter:

      Dear Sir—

At a meeting of the Young Ireland Club
(inner circle) it was carried unanimously
that you be removed at an early date
and that for reasons best nown to yourself.
So I write to warn you to prepare
to meet your god, and may the holly virgin
have mercy on your vile corpses
and salvation on your never-dying sole.
I am, your fore warner

      A. O'Bryan

Robert Ford Duff, a bottle blower, and his wife
went to Dr Bisset to get a death certificate for their child
but the doctor was not satisfied with their explanation
of an epilectic fit as cause of death.
He called the next day and examined the body
and concluded that the child's bruises could not be accounted
for by a fit—death had ensued from external violence.
He informed the police and in the course of enquiries
a witness was found who saw Duff kick an object three times,
which turned out to be his stepdaughter of four and a half years,
whom he had killed by beating, kicking and throwing over a fence.
It was said that Duff, being of a low, degraded nature, probably
had given excessive punishment.

Sergeant Morrison and two young officers
arrested Fullerton, fighting drunk,
and took him to the police station
through the thick of the gang.
Fullerton was charged
with assaulting Sergeant Morrison.
As each gang member gave evidence
came the constantly recurring phrase
'And then Big Tommy from the Toll hit me
and that's the last I remember.'
Eventually the magistrate asked
'Who is this Big Tommy from the Toll?
If he is in court will he please stand up?'
In complete silence Sergeant Morrison
got to his feet, bowed and sat down again.
The magistrate looked at the huge officer
and said 'I think I begin to understand.
Thank you, Sergeant Morrison.'

GLASGOW, C.1965

'I was sitting beside my wife
and not bothering anyone.
My feet were in the passageway
and the conductor asked me to get them in.
When I wouldn't, he kicked them in.
I waited till my wife was off the bus
then I hit him. I thought he deserved it.'

NOTES

p. 9 Dumfries, 1623
'brig-end'—bridge-end.

p. 10 Auldearn, Nairn, 1662
From the famous trial for witchcraft of Isobel Gowdie (1632-1662).

p. 2 Glasgow, 1685
The Tolbooth was a Glasgow Town Council building at Glasgow Cross used as a gaol in the 17th and 18th centuries. Only its tower remains.
'reset and converse'—handling of stolen goods with intention to sell

p. 13 Langside, near Glasgow, 1687
'dang'—knocked, struck

p. 15 Pollokshaws, 1784
'rive'—tear, rip

p. 19 Paisley, 1770
'tuck'—beat

p. 22 Edinburgh, 1826
There was a split in the Church of Scotland in 1733, with one party being known as Seceders. They, too, split in 1747 with a disagreement over the oath required of a town burgess [freeman] on taking office [the oath of Burghers]. The opposing Seceder groups became known as the Burghers and Anti-Burghers. Covenanters were originally those who subscribed to the National Covenant (1638) and Solemn League and Covenant (1643), by which they swore to uphold their chosen form of worship.

p. 28 Edinburgh, 1828
From the trial of William Burke who, with William Hare, murdered people to sell their bodies for dissection.

p. 37 Glasgow, 1853
The judge was the famous Henry Cockburn (1779-1854). He was the defence lawyer for Burke's wife in the trial for the Burke and Hare murders, and won her acquittal.

p. 38 Girvan, Ayrshire, 1854
'claes'—clothes

p. 40 Bothwell, 1879

'ben'—in through the house

'spunks'—matches

p. 43 Tayport, 1882

'butter-kit'—a container for butter

p. 44 Forfar, 1885

This references the strange old law that only 'bona fide travellers' could be served drink on a Sunday.

p. 45 Dundee, 1889

If Mr Bury's statement is true, this solves the mystery at last.

p. 49 Glasgow, c. 1930

Fullerton—William Fullerton (d.1962), the fascist leader of the Glasgow Billy Boys razor gang of the 1920s and 1930s (the eponymous 'King Billy' of Edwin Morgan's poem, written after Fullerton's death).

BIBLIOGRAPHY

Several books on Scottish history, transcripts of trials and the occasional old newspaper were consulted in preparing these poems, but principal sources were as follows:

Robert Pitcairn, *Ancient Criminal Trials in Scotland*. Vol. III, Part II (1615-1624). Edinburgh, 1833.

William Hector, *Selections from the Judicial Records of Renfrewshire ... in the seventeenth and eighteenth centuries*. Paisley, 1876.

David Syme, *Reports of Proceedings in the High Court of Justiciary from 1826 to 1829*. Edinburgh, 1829.

John Shaw, *Reports of Cases before the High Court and Circuit Courts of Justiciary in Scotland during the years 1848, 1849, 1850, 1851, 1852*. Edinburgh, 1853.

Reports of Cases before the High Court and Circuit Courts of Justiciary in Scotland during the years 1868-1870. Reprint by General Books, 2009.

Reports of Cases before the High Court and Circuit Courts of Justiciary in Scotland during the years 1868-1885. Reprint by General Books, 2012.

Reports of Cases before the High Court of Justiciary in Scotland from 1893 to 1916. 4 vols. Reprint by General Books, 2012.

Amy Mathieson, *Scottish Trials*. Glasgow, 2016.

George Saunders, *Casebook of the Bizarre: a review of famous Scottish trials*. Edinburgh, 1991.

Deborah A. Symonds, *Notorious Murders, Black Lanterns and Moveable Goods: the transformation of Edinburgh's underworld in the early nineteenth century*. Akron, Ohio, 2006.

[T. M. Tod], *Scottish Crime and Punishment: The Scots Black Kalendar*. Perth, 1938. New edition: Newtongrange, 1985.